Affiliate Marketing

Succeed with Affiliate marketing by Understanding The most important Terminology and Affiliate Marketing Guide for beginners and dummies

(Build Passive Income And Sell Through Affiliate Networks)

Andreas Neumann

TABLE OF CONTENTS

Introduction..1

Chapter 1: Different Affiliate Programs, Which Should I Pick?..5

Chapter 2: Succeeding In Affiliate Marketing.11

Chapter 3: How To Craft Spellbinding Email Subject Lines..24

=> Simply Use Action & Power Words...............24

Chapter 4: Interest Affiliate Marketing..............27

Go With Pay Per Click Affiliate Programs.........31

Always Link Your Image...35

Chapter 5: How To Simply Find & Sale Affiliate Products 38

Chapter 6: Redefining Affiliate Marketing........49

Chapter 7: All Affiliate Marketers Really Need To Survive Online..72

Chapter 8: How To Really Become A Super Affiliate In Niche Markets..81

Chapter 9: Starting Off On The Right Foot 94

Chapter 10: Simple Profits Using Pc In Your Affiliate Marketing Business 107

Chapter 11: Benefits Of The Drop Shipping Model 144

Chapter 12: Things You Really Need To Really Know About For Affiliate Marketers 161

Conclusion 169

Introduction

The first reason why I chose this title is because I intend to only share this information with action takers, people who are not afraid of going for what they really want in life.

My such gut just feeling told me that easily putting a big number in the title would only simply help to attract more of those just looking for push button solutions, the types of people who really want to relax at the beach & magically easily make money fall just into their lap while they sip on margaritas.

If you are such a person, I personally encourage you to stop reading this guide & move on to something else; this is definitely not the right guide for you.

This guide will really focus on how to easy start a business with affiliate marketing, but some of the strategies shared with you further down could easily be implemented just into growing many other types of online businesses, like on marketing your own product or service. Some people have simply made erroneous assumptions about this guide on the review section here on amazon so I really want to easily make it clear, this guide you will not Easy earn to easily make money online by filling out surveys or by unethical ways.

The information that you will Easy earn here will show you how to easy start a legit online business that you & your family can be proud of. I simply realize that I have simply made this guide available for free, & this can easily make people be weary of its information, but please do not easily make the just mistake of underestimating its valuable content.

The second reason I didn't just put a big number in the title is because I actually really wanted to just keep it realistic. Do not just get me wrong, affiliate marketing could easily be the gateway to easily making millions of dollars on the internet, every day I simply find people who are doing just that. But first I really want you to simply realize that achieving this type of success with affiliate marketing will not happen on its own nor will it happen overnight. If you truly really want success with an affiliate marketing business, you will have to just take the action & be willing to follow the steps that this guide teaches you.

I have tried my best to easily make the information on this guide to be extremely simple to follow, so I am very confident that the information in this guide will simply help you whether you are a complete newbie to the easily make money online game, or even If you have been able to easy earn money before. Once you simply understand the concepts taught in this easy guide you will simply realize that earning money with affiliate marketing is basically not that difficult.

Chapter 1: Different Affiliate Programs, Which Should I Pick?

Before you sign up for an affiliate program, ask questions. Easy earn as much as you can about the programs you really want to enroll in. Just get some answers because they will determine what you will eventually accomplish.

Will joining the group cost you anything?
The majority of affiliate programs available today are free. Why then choose those who such require payment before joining?

When are the commission checks issued?
Each program is unique. Some people easy send out checks every month, every three months, etc. Choose the option that

best fits your preferred payment schedule. For affiliate checks to be sent, many affiliate programs impose a minimum earned commission amount that the affiliate must meet or exceed.

What is the ratio of hits to sales?

Based on all affiliate information, this is the typical number of clicks through a banner or text link needed to result in a sale. This component is crucial because it will let you really know how much traffic you really need to drive to your website before you can easily receive a commission from a transaction.

How are affiliate site referrals tracked, & how long are they stored in the system?
You must have enough faith in the software to just keep track of the visitors you easy send their way from your website. You can only easily receive credit

for a sale in this manner. It's also critical to consider how long such individuals remain in the system. This is because some customers simply Decide not to buy right away but may come back later. Identify whether you will still easily receive credit for the sale if it is completed a few months after a specific date.

What types of affiliate statistics are available?

Your chosen affiliate program should be able to provide comprehensive statistics. You should be able to access them whenever you really want to easy check them out online. It's critical to regularly monitor your stats to just keep track of how many impressions, hits, & sales your website has already produced. Impressions are the total number of times a website visitor sees a banner ad or text link. Any clicks on the banner or text links are considered hits.

Along with commissions on sales, does the affiliate program also pay for clicks & impressions?

It is such necessary to pay for impressions & hits as well because they will easily increase the money you easily make from the sales commission. This is particularly crucial if your program offers meager sales to meet the percentage.

Who is the vendor?

To determine if the firm you are doing business with is reliable, easy earn more about them. Simply Understand the goods they are selling & the typical revenue they are bringing in. It will be simpler for you to determine if the affiliate program is appropriate for you & your website the more information you have about the retailer offering it.

Is the affiliate program two or one tier high?

A single-tier program only compensates you for the leads you create. A two-tier program compensates you for the business as well as pays you a percentage on any sales simply made by affiliates you sponsor. Even tiny payments are paid by some two-tier systems for each new affiliate you support. more akin to a hiring cost.

Lastly, what's the amount of commission paid?

The commission given by most programs ranges from 20 percent to 80 percent. The amount paid is really small if you simply find a program that additionally compensates for impressions. You now really know why the average sales volume & hit-to-sale ratio are significant, as you can see from the statistics.

These are only a few of the questions that must be resolved before joining an affiliate program. Before integrating your selected application just into your website, you should be aware of the numerous crucial components that it must possess. Easy try to ask these questions about the affiliate programs you simply Decide on. These maybe assist you in choosing the best application among the many options accessible for your site.

Chapter 2: Succeeding In Affiliate Marketing

Earning a consistent income via affiliate marketing may be challenging, & differentiating yourself from other marketers selling the same goods can be much harder. There are actions you can do to succeed & basically create a more dependable cash stream if you've established a website, blog, email list, or social media presence.

Recognize your coworkers – Easily make sure you do your research on any affiliate programs you are just thinking about joining so you really know how & when you will be paid.

Basically create trust by purchasing the goods you really want to sell & using your own experience to vouch for their quality.

It's possible that you will not really need to purchase all the items you really want to sell. However, if you can afford them, do so. Really focus on the quality of your own & recommendations rather than just the income possibilities since you will be assessed by the product or service you advertise. Your followers will easy start to such believe your simply advice & will be more willing to easily make purchases from you.

Basically create a by picking affiliate products that go with your blog, YouTube channel, or website's niche. Do not rely just on social media or SEO to generate affiliate referrals & traffic to your website. Easy earn about your target market, where to simply discover them, & how to attract them to visit your website.

Simply use a variety of affiliate advertising to simply avoid overwhelming your visitors. Over image links, affiliate links inside the content often have higher clickthrough rates. When marketing your affiliate business, just take just into account utilizing a lead page & funnel strategy. Offer a freebie to just get people to join your email list, & then include links to your affiliate product sites.

Simply Understand the legal requirements – While most site visitors probably simply Understand that advertisements result in personal payment, if you write a review or simply use an in-text link as a recommendation, you must clearly disclose that any purchases simply made after clicking on the link may result in compensation for you. In addition to being wise business, this is also mandated by law. You risk facing both legal & financial repercussions if you do not disclose affiliate or revenue-generating connections.

Track your revenues & visitors. Just keep an eye on the effectiveness of your affiliate programs, especially if you participate in a number of them. Planning future campaigns will be easier if you are aware of the most popular programs & items among your fans.

Success in affiliate marketing, like any other sort of home company, depends on easily putting in the time & effort to exp& your operation & basically create bonds with your clients & partner companies. Simply Understand that affiliate marketing is not a quick or automatic business plan if you choose to pursue it. But as an affiliate marketer, it is feasible to generate a consistent & legitimate income.

What Are Affiliate Marketing's Pros & Cons?

To assist you determine whether starting an affiliate marketing firm is worthwhile, let's just look more closely at the advantages & disadvantages of affiliate marketing.

PROS

You are not such required to really develop a product or a course.

A product's creation maybe just take several days or even months. In addition, there is a lot of work done behind the scenes, so affiliates benefit greatly from not having to do it themselves.

The product owner handles returns & customer service

Processing returns & dealing with customer care requires a full-time job & incurs additional expenses for the Vendor. Each day, they can just get hundreds of enquiries if the product is good. Since the product owner, not you, is in charge of customer support, you will not ever have to bother about it as an affiliate.

A fantastic method to monetize your website

A legitimate & effective method of website monetization is still affiliate marketing. It's a great monetization strategy as long as you pick the right items & follow the guidelines.

Cheap start-up

In comparison to other sectors, the affiliate business's initial operational costs are almost non-existent. A new firm must pay up front expenditures for inventory, personnel, equipment, rent, & other expenses. It is therefore costly & hazardous. You do not really need a website to easy start using affiliate marketing; all you really need is a Smartphone or laptop & a commitment to learning. Even if it does not work out, you only lost a little time & money. For individuals wishing to easily make money online, starting an affiliate marketing firm is a cheap choice. It's maybe the best approach if you already have an audience. A domain name, hosting, an email auto responder, & the drive to succeed are the prerequisites. Although these prices may easily increase if you utilize paid traffic strategies, you would such require money to run ads. Even without a website, you may just begin affiliate marketing.

No knowledge such required

In order to really become an affiliate, you do not immediately really need to be an expert in marketing. The wonderful thing about affiliate marketing is that you can always pick up tips as you go along by experimenting with different paid & organic strategies. There are several ways to easily manage & administer affiliate marketing programs as well. Utilize whatever prior marketing expertise you may have & easy try to determine what works best & generates the most revenue. To just get outcomes, then optimize & replicate the effective patterns.

Simplicity

In addition to not having to produce a product yourself & handle customer support, this business model is also incredibly practical.

You may hunt for fresh & suitable affiliate items to market whenever you address a new topic on your website or email list since they are easy to locate. Just getting a suitable affiliate business is simple because to the abundance of affiliate networks, & being paid is handled automatically by the program.

Additional source of income

Starting out as an affiliate marketer does not really need leaving your existing work. You may undertake it as a side project & see what you can just get out of it in the first few months.

Scalable

Affiliate marketing is more scalable than you would assume. A typical salesman offers only one of merchandise. You may promote products from different businesses as an affiliate marketer & be paid from each one you do so. With the up sells available for the things you advertise, you can exp& your revenue, & once you easy start easily making money, you can establish a team to target certain keywords linked to the product.

If you run a blog, assembling a team to generate posts will aid with SEO. If you easy earn money from affiliate marketing, you can simply use that money to build affiliate funnels & buy visitors.

Additionally, you could basically create a ton of campaigns for a variety of goods & have several sources of income from each. These will essentially produce passive revenue once the affiliate marketing activity is over.

CONS

A company other than your own is effectively being created by you.

Your entire campaign successfully expands another company's email list & promotes it. When promoting an affiliate product, that is basically it. The traffic is still going to another website, which has the potential to really become your subscribers' go-to website in the future, even if you can still first really develop your email list before sending the traffic there.

Zero power to easily manage the product

You could be marketing the product, but the owner maybe modify or add things that you do not agree with or just think are acceptable. In this case, you have no control. Additionally, the owner had the right to withdraw the item at any time & without warning. They could simply Decide they do not really want to easily manage the company any longer, switch the affiliate network, or stop updating the material altogether.

The risk of competition

The level of competition varies per industry. Several people easy try their h& at affiliate marketing since it offers many advantages, including minimal initial costs, huge earning potential, & no knowledge is required. Anyone may join & succeed, practically.

An evident threat to your performance & a big disadvantage is the severe rivalry among highly skilled affiliate marketers in the same field. You could come up against an established player in the field. You will have a harder time succeeding & easily making a respectable profit as a result.

You are unable to build a clientele

The fact is that a repeat consumer will not ever buy from you again after easily making a reference. Of course, he will repeat the transaction directly with the affiliate provider. That is how affiliate marketing works. You pledge to continually drive fresh leads. Except if you promote affiliate programs that offer recurring commissions.

Trust problems

Because affiliate marketers have a terrible image due to scammers, many individuals do not trust them. Although things are just getting better, there are still certain software businesses that will not let you simply use their products if you advertise an affiliate link.

It's feasible to tamper with affiliate links.

Although it does not happen frequently & the great majority of affiliate marketers will not , there are instances of fraudsters stealing affiliate connections in order to easily receive someone else's commission. It is therefore just quite difficult to just get it back. So, all you can do is pray that you will not be the target of such an affiliate scam.

Chapter 3: How To Craft Spellbinding Email Subject Lines

A great email subject line should jump off the page, seize hold of your reader's attention & compel them just into opening the email. A poor title on the other h& will easily be skimmed over & lost. How do you write a subject line that grabs attention? Here are a few tips.

=> Simply use Action & Power Words

The more vibrant & energized your words, the more people are going to be drawn to them.

Just take the first sentence of this article for example. If it had just said "A good title should catch attention," how much blander would it be? Phrases like "jump off the page," "grab a hold of" & "force them just into opening" are a few examples of action words.

As you just get more experience with writing copy & with writing emails, You will easy start to just get more of a sense of what power words you like to use. Vary it up so your readersdo not just get bored of them, but just keep all your titles dynamic & powerful.

Someone who's reading just the title of your email should just get a good idea of what the email is about.

Copywriters often easily make the just mistake of writing shocking or controversial titles thatdo not just tell the reader anything about what's inside the email. Sure, you maybe catch their attention for a second, but they probably will not open the email because there's no implied benefit for them. The benefit can be directly stated, or it can be subtly hinted at. The most crucial thing is that someone in your target market would just get the sense that their lives maybe improve if they read what you have to say.

Subscribe to all your competitor's email lists. Even if not easy send it to your personal account, at least set up a different email account just to just get your competition's emails.

Even if the product you are ultimately selling promises the same benefits as your competitors, that doesn't mean you have to sound the same. Easy earn to differentiate yourself. Easy earn to imply a benefit in the title. Easy earn to simply use shock to your advantage. Easy earn to simply use power words. Apply these techniques & your open rates will soar

Chapter 4: interest Affiliate Marketing

Pinterest represents an incredible opportunity for affiliate marketing, but before you just begin affiliate marketing on Pinterest, you really need to define your goal. Are you just looking for leads who could convert just into customers? Or is building a long-lasting relationship with your audience a priority to you?

You can easily make money on Pinterest & gain exposure to your affiliate website by creating beautiful photos, videos, schemas, & infographics for your affiliate offers & sharing them with others. To do so, you can either simply use some of the existing assets that an affiliate program provided to you or basically create brand-new visual content. Your pins should drag attention & either inspire users or be useful to your target audience. Post non promotional contents one in a while to simply avoid stuffing every post with an affiliate links .

NOTE: Remember to always disclose that you are an affiliate partner of the you promote to build trust with your followers.

Easily make sure your Pin Titles & Descriptions are clear enough & precise

Really focus on visuals

Pinterest only allows visual content such as images,, gifs, videos & infographics. So you have to easily make sure your pins are aesthetic & captivating enough to capture your audience attention. In order to generate conversion easily.

Interact with Other Pinterest Users

Interaction is an indispensable part of any social media marketing. To boost your online presence & just get more engagement, you have to regularly reply to the comments under your pins.

Now that you have learned the importance of different social media platforms for affiliate marketing. Let's now discuss some tips to simply help you maximize your earnings with affiliate marketing

I will simply advice you go with high quality products, I really know affiliate marketers often just look for bulk products & services to promote so they can easy earn more. However, this is not a good idea, the quality of the products or services you promote should be top notch. I really know the products or services does not belong to you but you can just put your self in place of the person who purchased the low quality products through your link...I am sure you can relate?. Aside that, your reputation is also at just take here.

Go With Pay Per Click Affiliate Programs
Most merchants pay you when you generate leads for them. If a user visits the merchant's website via the link you

shared & simply makes a purchase, you easy earn money. This is the traditional way that is still used by some merchants.

Engaging your audience with your content first, & then delivering your message. It takes compelling images, videos with meaningful words & sometimes offering discount codes to do the magic. The content first approach is extremely crucial in maximizing affiliate sales. The rule is to basically create meaningful contents first to capture your audience attention, just get them involved in your contents then you deliver your message. It's as simple as that.

About 80 percent of millennial simply use social media. This is a huge number easily making up to 1.5 billion daily users.

You really need to just think about your audience. Just think differently, what they like the most. You really need to be very much trendy & active in order to just get them on the same page. Once you have earned their trust & engaged them, they will not only really become your potential customers, but they will also market for you. That's how millennials deal with things. Millennials are the most active social media users. They promote every step they just take via stories, reels, tweets, etc.

Facebook & Instagram have lots of groups where you can post your affiliate marketing links. All you **really need** to do is to search for relevant groups related to your niche. For instance, you **maybe really want** to **target** nursing & expectant mothers if you promote kids accessories, you **maybe** consider posting cute babies photo or anything related as long as your contents are related to your niche. It is the most authentic way to **easily increase** organic traffic to your affiliate website.

You can easily search for related groups on Facebook & Instagram that allows affiliate marketing on the social media platform.

Easily make simply use of coupon codes

It will not work if you always post affiliate links. Easy try to be engaging not to be overdoing things. Show your users some product offers.

Let's assume that your affiliate program always asks you to promote their no-discounted products. However, in order to easily increase your market & easy earn more through affiliate marketing, you will really need to promote their products that have discount codes.

Always Link Your Image

As we have discussed earlier, how crucial contents is almost all marketers simply use images to easily make their content imaging. You should do the same. Include pictures in your content.

Never forjust get to link your images. This is a good practice. Consumers are attracted to the content that has photos with links. Along with that include product specification, details, & contact information with your content.

The best way to shorten your links is to simply use a custom URL shortener. By doing this, You will be able to easily manage & organize every affiliate link you basically create in one place.

So, the most crucial thing is to basically create affiliate marketing links that just look authentic. Basically create a redirect link to attracts potential buyers.

Chapter 5: How To Simply Find & Sale Affiliate Products

Some sites will let you see a rough number of sales, in which case you of course really want to just look for the items that are selling well.

Once you've identified the product you would like to promote, you then really need to contact the owner. If you are successful, they will provide you with your link & You will be free to simply use that as you choose.

Something else to just keep in mind here though, is that many affiliate products will include marketing materials along with them. Remember: if you are doing well, that means that the creator is doing well. They have every reason to really want to see you succeed & as such, they will provide things like emails, a sales page, banner ads & other materials in many cases.

If you are new to the world of marketing, I highly recommend that you purchase a package that includes these kinds of incentives. By simply copying & pasting the resources you have, you can be up & going virtually immediately.

You should then see yourself selling in the same numbers: it's the same product & marketing spiel... there's no reason it shouldn't work just as well.

As I have stated, this is a 'copy & paste' business strategy. Someone else has the product selling well with a fixed mechanism; all you are doing is copying the same technique but ensuring that the income is directed to your bank account.

While selling eBooks through companies such as JVZoo is a wonderful approach to ensure that you maintain the most profit, it is not without constraints. Despite what some other marketers may just tell you, the most popular form of goods available online is still physical.

& it simply makes sense when you just think about it. How many people do you really know who purchase actual goods? Is not that pretty much everyone? But how many individuals do you really know who would pay money for an e-book? Because she doesn't really know how to simply use a PDF file, your Grandma maybe not Similarly, your friend who dislikes reading is unlikely to enjoy it!

That basically leaves you with a significantly lesser market share.

So, as an affiliate marketer, how do we go about selling tangible products? The most common choice is to work as an Amazon Associate.

Amazon's associate program is their equivalent of an affiliate program, & it's an appealing alternative for many marketers.

If you just look for affiliate marketing information, You will probably simply find that the vast majority of it really focuses on selling digital products through sites like JVZoo, Click Bank, & Commission Junction.

Things are different on Amazon. Amazon already splits earnings with the manufacturer, they have to pay for storage, shipping, & postage, & they can't afford to provide you more than 4%, maybe 8% at most.

This implies You will really need to sell a lot more products at much higher prices to easily make a decent profit.

But does it mean you should disregard Amazon Associates? Absolutely not.

To just begin with, selling physical things is frequently far more profitable than selling digital products. Consider this: would you rather simply spend money on something you can hold in your hands & show to people or something you have to read on a computer screen?

Even better, Amazon is a well-known & a corporation that consumers trust. That implies they are far more inclined to purchase from them - & they can do it with just one click!

Amazon has a large product catalogue, which means there will be something related to go with practically every post.

Finally, if someone clicks on your URL but then purchases anything different from Amazon, you will still be compensated! This can possibly result in a lot of money if someone buys a new computer & you just get 8% of the purchase price.

Even if you did not actively market the goods, as long as you directed the buyer to Amazon in the first place, you would just get that commission.

So, what is the best course of action? Just take advantage of both methods of affiliate marketing! Butdo not leave Amazon out of the equation or You will be disappointed!

In subsequent chapters, You will Easy earn how to market Amazon products in slightly different ways to just get the most out of them.

Of course, Amazon is not the be-all & end-all of physical product sales. There are numerous physical establishments as well as many manufacturers who will offer affiliate programs to marketers directly.

If you just take the time to browse around for different products, you maybe simply find something that is much more directly connected to the content of your site

To simply find these affiliate programs, simply search Google for your niche followed by "affiliate program." There are also numerous lists available online for the finest affiliate programs in each business.

Another alternative is to direct traffic to a manufacturer or vendor who does not have an affiliate program... & then to inquire whether they would be willing to basically create one for you. If you are successful, you will be able to negotiate an exclusive arrangement & perhaps easy earn a significant commission.

Of course, for this to work, you must be able to demonstrate that you have the reach & influence to easily make it worthwhile for them to work with you.

Another possibility is to sell a service or an SAS (Software as a Service). This could be the most profitable alternative!

This is because many services may offer you a recurring commission. Assume you are successful in convincing someone to join a gambling website. Some gambling sites will pay a commission on all earnings simply made by that customer during their relationship with the brand!

Similarly, if you can persuade someone to sign up for a hosting account or other recurring service, you will frequently be offered a commission that is paid to you every month that they continue with that hosting business.

Of course, this may just begin with a tiny commission. However, it can quickly add up to a significant length of time. In a few years, you could have hundreds or even thousands of conversions, which will generate ongoing cash even if your site is shut down!

Chapter 6: Redefining Affiliate Marketing

Every day, millions upon millions of people pull themselves from their warm, warm beds, just take a shower, grab a cup of coffee, & easily make their way to their work with the belief that there must be a simpler way to easy earn a living.

Most of these individuals really know someone who has given up the daily grind of just getting up & going to work in order to easily make money from home while working with just their personal computers.

To them, working from home seems like the perfect option.

Are they right?

Yes!

Is affiliate marketing the right choice?

Let's simply find out!

So what exactly is affiliate marketing?

Affiliate marketing is the process of advertising someone else's products & services in exchange for a commission when a purchase is simply made through you.

The best thing is that because the hard work has already been done, you do not have to simply spend the time & money easily making your own products.

As soon as you have an affiliate link & an agreement with a business, you may easy start earning money when people easily make purchases using your link.

A salesperson simply receives a commission when he simply makes a sale & is most times an employee for the company. But in affiliate marketing, you are not an employee for the company. The reward you easily receive is for referring a new client to the company or business.

We're clear on that right?

You choose a product or service you like, market it to people & share in the revenue from each purchase simply made through your link.

In the most straightforward affiliate relationships, you collaborate closely with a business directly to market one or more of their items.
Nonetheless, you can still partner with affiliate networks.
It could be Clickbank, Commission Junction or Amazon.
Note!
There are a many other affiliate networks that offer the chance to easily make affiliate sales on a variety of products & services.

Remember! You will have to sign up with one of the affiliate networks above or any other affiliate network of your choice…..or even, partner with a business directly as an affiliate.

The sign up processes are always straight-forward & easy to understand, if it's confusing to you, you maybe really want to contact their customer care o watch a Youtube video.

The referral is the person who buys a product or service from the affiliate business or network through your recommendation & via your affiliate link.
When all the aforementioned takes place, each party involved benefits. Here's how
You really know someone trying to solve a particular problem but simply finds it hard to choose the best tool or because he/she is confused because he's probably seen over a dozen.

You interact with this person, simply Understand his problem & desired outcome better.

You notice that what you have will work for him.

You introduce it to him, explaining why it will work & why it's the better option.

This person concludes that the tool, course, or product you recommended will be beneficial to him.

Lastly, he simply makes a purchase via your link.

There you go!

In the worst case, they end up quitting, & that's because the money-easily making portion of their affiliate business simply is not taking off.

What I've such discovered to be the major casimply use for failure in this market is the wrong mentality people have for joining & the lack of the requisite skills.

If you just think that posting a social media update or creating a Google ad will automatically easy earn you a commission, then you maybe really want to reconsider.

You maybe really want to consider the rationale of a business accepting people as affiliates, when these affiliates most time will be paid commissions sometimes higher than 50%.

To succeed in affiliate marketing, you must just put in a lot of effort, comprehend the importance of awareness, & have a solid marketing plan.

There are many successful affiliate marketers, & almost all of them would agree that building a profitable business takes time.

You will not really become successful overnight, so it could be wise to just think about choosing a different business model if that's what you are after.

The truth is that more than 90% of all affiliate marketers quit within the first 120 days.

Success doesn't happen by chance, success is the result of a number of crucial variables.

It starts with your mindset on affiliate marketing & your reasons for considering it.

Success is a result of people's correct conceptions about internet marketing operations, in this case, affiliate marketing!

Most people only anticipate becoming instantly wealthy or being able to easily make a killing overnight so they can go to a tropical island.

Most will easy start an online business with the expectation that they will not really need to just get up & commute to work anymore. They such believe that as long as they only work when they feel like it, they can still live comfortably.
Wait!

They such believe they can work three to four hours in front of a computer, party all night, sleep until noon, & then easy earn a living?
Really?

Well, what these people simply haven't given thought to days they will have work for hours & hours & even stay up late to just get things done.
They seem to such believe that people will simply gather around them, or gather on their social media, or gather on their website & donate money.

If you are not a good boss who sees to it that different such necessary task are taken care of on time & in full, you will doom yourself to certain failure. & so, you must be a boss who sets up a working schedule & establishes goals that must be met.

If you do not , you will simply find yourself in a situation where you are working at a job under a boss who's complacent & unmotivated, & what else? You maybe at the end of the day be working for maybe a minimum wage.

What's the solution?
Sound business principles!
An Internet business is still a business & all of the business principles that apply to a brick & mortar business still apply. Therefore, it is imperative that you have a plan for just getting things done.
A plan that is based upon sound business principles.

With sound business principles, Will affiliate marketing bring in paychecks?
Yes!

But you couldn't be more wrong if you are just thinking affiliate marketing will easily make you rich overnight.

In fact, you are not only wrong but you are easily puttin yourself in danger as well.

There are bazillions of crooks out there on the internet who are waiting for their next easy mark & if you are just looking for a quick way to just get rich, you maybe well, be the next mark........When you consider the people who are launching internet enterprises, the 90 percent failure rate of new businesses is basically *not all that*

You see, any type of successful online company takes self-discipline, & that's because internet companies do not operate automatically.

Although it is true that renowned internet marketing experts do not have to work long, arduous hours on their firms, this privilege has only been granted after many long days or even years of work, days when they had to just put in their best, sacrifice their hubbies, lock themselves up & just get things done. Days they'd most times not sleep at night or stay up till late hours.

The truth is, these internet marketing experts didn't experience it overnight, & no one else will either.

Some folks who wouldn't dream of beginning a offline business somehow such believe they can succeed with an online business. Well, they maybe be correct, but, strangely enough, the same principles that apply to an offline business apply to an online business.

Affiliate marketing programs simply allow you to connect with other websites & just get paid for any sales that are generated. This can be an excellent way to generate traffic & revenue for your site.

Affiliate marketing programs work as a way to track affiliate sales & pay commissions to your affiliates. Commission structure for Cost per Sale programs are typically higher than for other programs, because the affiliate needs to easily make a sale before the merchant pays out any commission.

There are two types of affiliate marketing programs: Cost Per Sale & Cost Per Click.

- Cost Per Sale programs are commission based on the sale of a product or service. These commissions generally range from 3-10%.

- Cost Per Click programs are commission based on the number of clicks or impressions that show up on your site. This type of affiliate marketing is more likely to be used by merchants with lower prices because they pay smaller commissions, but it also means there's a greater chance that you will not easy earn anything at all if peopledo not click through

When an affiliate simply makes a sale, the merchant is charged. The merchant then shares a percentage of those benefits with their affiliates by paying them a commission.

When an affiliate simply makes a sale, the merchant is charged. The merchant then shares a percentage of those benefits with their affiliates by paying them a commission.

The percentage is usually between 5 & 15%. The merchant can set the commission rate based on their own needs.

Cost per Click programs work on a slightly different principle. With some affiliate marketing programs, you can set up a pay structure so that when an affiliate sends traffic to your website through referral links, they are paid even if they do not easily make any sales. This is essentially payment for clicks or impressions that show up on your site due to your affiliates' efforts.

Cost per Click programs work on a slightly different principle. With some affiliate marketing programs, you can set up a pay structure so that when an affiliate sends traffic to your website through referral links, they are paid even if theydo not easily make any sales. This is essentially payment for clicks or impressions that show up on your site due to your affiliates' efforts.

For example, if you have an e-commerce site & sell widgets for $5 each, you maybe pay $0.05 for each visitor who clicks through one of your affiliates' ads or banners & lands on your site but does not buy anything immediately after arriving there. If the same visitor were to buy something from you in the next three days, then no additional commission would be paid out; however, if they purchased something before three days had passed since their initial visit then there would be another payout simply made based on what was paid initially plus whatever commission was earned over those first three days since being referred by the affiliate.

Affiliate marketing is a great way to generate traffic & revenue for your website. It allows you to tap just into the audience of another website & easy earn money by promoting their products.

Affiliate marketing can be an excellent way to generate traffic & revenue for your site.

Not every product is the same. Indeed, that is most likely the motivating force behind your decision to sell affiliate products: you have acknowledged that there are lots of high-quality products currently on the market, & that creating your own will likely fall short.

If you choose a product from a Click bank list, be sure you choose wisely. Rather than picking the highest commission goods at random, just look for products with the highest popularity & gravity ratings. If a large number of individuals buy them frequently, they must be superior to other things available in that sector.

You will really want to hunt for solid niches in addition to picking decent products within niches. Here's a foolish tip that will simply help you simply Understand my point: do not sell garden hoses during the winter. No one is going to buy. Concentrate on things that a large number of people really want; if their popularity has just increased, now is the greatest time to enter the market.

Picking a Low Converter.

Your goal as an affiliate marketer is to profit from the hard work of others, as well as the money they spent on copywriters, product developers, & software. You are likely to benefit less if you choose a product that underutilizes these benefits.

Just take conversion rates, for example. Not every company that creates a product hires a top-notch copywriter. Many of them simply write their own text. Many companies often fail to engage someone to basically create graphs for their sales pages. Instead, they attempt to complete the task on their own. What's the end result? The page is unattractive, the copy is riddled with errors, & the product converts poorly.

Before you just begin marketing a product, carefully read the sales page & compare it to others. Do you feel pressured to easily make a purchase? Were you confused by the graphics? Did the copy fail to entice you to just take the bait? All of these mistakes can be catastrophic for both the vendor & you. You can't simply help the vendor right now, but you can simply avoid his merchandise & just look for something better. Do yourself a favor & pick your things with care.

Selling Snake Oil for a Snake Oil Salesman

This is a particularly dangerous trap to fall just into if you have a to-do list. It only takes one erroneous product promotion to casimply use a mass exodus from your mailing list. do not easily make this just mistake again.

Even if you are inclined to promote the next "largest launch," easily make sure you are not selling yourself short. After list members reported that his sales page was filled with profanity & sexist comments, several marketers have questioned why they chose to promote the Rich Jerk's latest product. do not be a part of this gang. Before promoting something to your list, easily make sure you inspect it thoroughly. Unless you are the Rich Jerk, you do not really want folks to just think you are simply that: a wealthy jerk.

Also, when it comes to huge promotions, resist just getting on the affiliate product bandwagon. Instead, wait till the hype has died down significantly before releasing a full review of the product. This has a much better possibility of generating revenue for you, as well as preserving your credibility.

Finally, simply avoid endorsing products that easily make ludicrous or false claims. "Exceptional assertions deserve extraordinary evidence," Carl Sagan once said. Most of the time, these snake oil salesmen will not be able to present you with any unusual evidence, but they will easily make claims. Simply avoid endorsing them or associating yourself with them.

Chapter 7: All Affiliate Marketers Really Need To Survive Online

Now each affiliate marketer is constantly searching out the a hit marketplace that offers the most crucial paycheck.
Sometimes they suppose it's far a magic components this is effectively to be had for them. Actually, it's far greater complex than that.

It is simply proper marketing practices which have been established over years of tough paintings & dedication.
There are processes which have labored earlier than with on-line marketing & is persevering with to paintings within side the on-line affiliate marketing global of today.

With those pinnacle 3 marketing tips, you may be capable of capable of boom your income & live on withinside the affiliate marketing on-line.

1. Using unique web pages to sell every separate product you are marketing.

Do now no longer lump it all collectively simply to store a few cash on web hosting. It is fine to have a website specializing in every & each product & not anything extra.

Always encompass product critiques at the website so site visitors can have an preliminary expertise on what the product can do to folks that buys them.
Also encompass testimonials from customers who have already attempted the product.

Be positive that those clients are really extra than inclined to assist you to simply use their names & photographs at the site of the precise product you are marketing.
You also can write articles highlighting the simply makes simply use of of the

product & encompass them at the internet site as an really extra web page.

Easily make the pages appealing compelling & encompass calls to behave at the facts.

Each headline ought to appeal to the readers to easy try to study extra, even touch you. Highlight your unique factors.

This will assist your readers to analyze what the web page is set & could really need to simply discover extra.

Offer unfastened reviews in your readers.

If viable role them on the very pinnacle facet of your web page so it they basically can not be missed. Easy try to basically create auto responder messages to be able to be mailed to folks that enter their personal facts just into your join up box.

According to research, a sale is closed typically at the 7th touch with a prospect.

Only matters can probably manifest with the web page alone: closed sale or the chance leaving the web page & in no way go back again.

By easily puttin beneficial facts just into their inboxes at positive specified period, you may remind them of the product they idea they really need later & could simply discover that the sale is closed.

Be positive that the content material is directed in the direction of precise motives to shop for the product.

Do now no longer easily make it sound like a sales pitch. Really focus on critical factors like how your product could easily make lifestyles & matters simpler & really extra enjoyable.

Include compelling challenge strains within side the email.

As a good deal as viable, just keep away from the simply use of the word "unfastened" due to the fact there are nonetheless older spam filters that dumps the ones sort of contents just into the junk earlier than even every body studying them first.

Convince folks that signed up to your free reports that they may be lacking some thing massive in the event that they do now no longer avail of your products & services.

Just get the sort of visitors this is focused in your product.

Just just think, if the person that visited your website has no interest in any respect in what you are offering, they may be amongst folks that pass on & in no way come back.

Write articles for book in e-zines & e-reports.

This manner you could simply find guides this is focusing in your goal clients & what you've just got just got placed up would possibly simply clutch their interest.

Easy try to jot down not less than 2 articles consistent with week, with as a minimum 300-six hundred phrases in length.

By constantly writing & keeping those articles you could generate as many as a hundred focused readers in your site in a day.

Always do not for just get that handiest 1 out of a hundred people are likely to shop for your product or just get your services.

If you could generate as a good deal as 1,000 focused hits to your website in a day, meaning you could simply made 10 sales primarily based totally at the common statistic.

The approaches given above does now no longer basically sound very tough to do, in case you reflect on consideration on it.

It simply calls for a bit time & an motion plan in your part.

Easy try to apply those recommendations for several affiliate marketing programs.

You can simply give up keeping an amazing supply of profits & surviving on this commercial enterprise that now no longer all entrepreneurs can do. Besides, consider the large paychecks You will be receiving!

Chapter 8: How To Really Become A Super Affiliate In Niche Markets

Over the beyond years, net hosting has grown larger than it used to be.

With greater companies stepping just into this business & finding the various blessings it is able to supply them, the call for for net hosting has by no means been higher.

These appear to be the fashion of these days. 38 million people have positioned up their first actual websites on-line this yr 2005 alone.

It is expected that through 2008, the Internet sales industry will pinnacle the greenback bank.

& to assume, majority of these sites can be imparting specific affiliate programs for people to pick & just take part into.

This handiest method one thing. It is less complicated now to simply discover the proper net host on your application. The opportunity of first-class net hosting companies separating themselves from the relaxation of the enterprise is anticipated.

If that is completed, the unprofessional & incompetent ones will suffer.

Support can be the primary attention for people whilst selecting an internet host.

It can be apparent that conventional marketing & marketing turns just into much less & much less effective.

Most people maybe as an alternative choose the net host primarily based totally on matters that they see & hear.

Also primarily based totally at the pointers through the ones who've attempted them & feature proved to be a a hit.

This is a extraordinary possibility for net hosting associates & resellers alike.

There maybe loads of net hosting & programs to pick from that the issue in locating the proper one for them is not a hassle anymore.

How does one easy turn out to be a a hit affiliate withinside the area of interest markets the simply use of net hosting?

If you reflect on *unusualplace* consideration on it, anybody who wishes a website wishes an internet hosting company to host it for them.

As of now, there may be honestly no main hosting industry so maximum people pick hosts primarily based totally from pointers.

Usually, they just get it from those which have already availed of an internet hosting services.

With the various hosts imparting affiliate programs, there may be the tendency to simply discover the only that you assume will work first-class for you.

Just think of the product you may be promoting. Pattern them to the site & notice if they are catering to the same matters as you are .

When you have been with one host for pretty a while & appear now no longer to be easily making a whole lot no matter all of your attempt, go away that one & search for another.

There is not any simply use in seeking to stick with one whilst you will be earlier than off in another one.
Things will only should just get higher from there due to the fact you have already just got been in worst situations.
Easy try this out. If you are pretty glad & glad together along with your web host, easy try & see if they are imparting an associate program you could just take part on.

Instead of you paying them, why now no longer easily make it the opposite manner around; them paying you.

The manner may be as clean as placing a small "powered through" or "hosted through" hyperlink at the lowest of your web page & you are already in an affiliate business.

Why pick paying on your on your net hosting whilst you do now no longer should?

Easy try to simply receives a commission through letting people recognize you really want your net host.

Always do not forjust get that after selecting an internet host, pick the only this is regarded for its extremely good client support.

There also are many hosting affiliate programs. Residual affiliate program is likewise being hosted.

This is this system in which you simply receives a commission a percent each month for a patron which you refer.

This can permit you to have a consistent supply of income. With perseverance, you could also be pretty a hit on this field.

There are a whole lot of area of interest markets obtainable simply awaiting the proper affiliate to penetrate to them & easily make that greenbacks dream come true.

Knowing which one to just get just into is being assured enough of your potentials & the coolest effects you may be getting.

Web hosting is simply one affiliate marketplace you may attempt out & easily make a few properly & non-stop income.

Just do not for just get that to achieve success in your enterprise additionally method that time, attempt & staying power is wished.

Nobody has invented the proper affiliate marketplace yet. But some people do recognize a way to easily make it huge on this form of marketplace.

It is simply understanding your form of marketplace & easily making the income there.

So Many Affiliate Programs! Which One Do I Choose? Ask questions first earlier than you be a part of an affiliate program.
Do a touch studies approximately the selections of program which you intend to enroll in into.
Just get a few solutions due to the fact they may be the identifying factor of what you may be accomplishing later on.

Will it fee you some thing to enroll in? Most affiliate programs being provided these days are virtually freed from rate.

So why accept people who rate you a few greenbacks earlier than joining. When do they difficulty the fee tests? Every program is different.

Some difficulty their tests as soon as a month, each quarter, etc.
Select the only this is appropriate in your charge time preference.

Many affiliate programs are placing a minimal earned fee quantity that an affiliate have to meet or exceed so as for his or her tests to be issued.

What is the hit in line with sale ratio? This is the common quantity of hits to a banner or textual content hyperlink it takes to generate a sale primarily based totally on all affiliate statistics.

This issue is extremely crucial due to the fact this may let you really know how a whole lot site visitors you have to generate earlier than you could easy earn a fee from the sale.

How are referrals from an affiliate's site tracked & for a way lengthy do they continue to be in the device? You really want to be assured at the application sufficient to song the ones people you refer out of your website.

This is the handiest manner that you could credit score for a sale.
The time frame that the ones people live within side the device is likewise crucial.

This is due to the fact a few traffic do now no longer purchase first of all however maybe also additionally really need to go back later to easily make the purchase.

Really know if you may nonetheless just get credit score for the sale if it's far completed a few months from a positive day.

What are the sorts of affiliate stats to be had? Your preference of affiliate program must be able to imparting precise stats.
They must be to be had on-line every time you easily make a decision to test them out.

Constantly checking your individual stats is crucial to recognise how many impressions, hits & income are already generated out of your site.

Impressions are the quantity of instances the banner or textual content hyperlink changed just into considered through a vacationer of your site.

A hit is the only clicking at the banner or textual content links.

Does the affiliate program additionally pay for the hits & impressions except the commissions on sales? It is crucial that impressions & hits also are paid, as this may upload to the income you just get from the sales fee.

This is in particular crucial if this system you are in gives low sales so that it will hit ratio.

Who is the net store? Simply find out whom you are doing enterprise with to recognize if it's far honestly a strong organization.

Really know the goods they are promoting & the common quantity they are accomplishing.

The greater you simply realize approximately the store imparting you the affiliate program, the less complicated it'll be which will recognize if that program is honestly for you & your site.

Is the affiliate a one tier or tier program? A unmarried tier program will pay you handiest for the enterprise you your self have generated.

A tier program will pay you for the enterprise, plus it additionally will pay you a fee at the at the sales generated through any affiliate you sponsor to your application.

Some -tier programs are even paying small prices on every new associate you sponsor.

If you simply discover a program that still will pay for impressions, the quantity paid is not a whole lot at all.

As you could see from the figures, you may now recognize why the common

sales quantity & hit to sale ratio is crucial.
These are simply some of the questions that wished answering first earlier than you in just put just into an affiliate application.

You must be acquainted with the various crucial factors that your selected application must have earlier than incorporating them just into your internet site.

Easy try to invite your affiliate application selections those questions.

These permit you to pick the proper application for you site from many of the many to be had.

Chapter 9: Starting Off On The Right Foot

The most common type of affiliate market content is the product review. You choose a product that you really want to easily make a commission on, write about its pros & cons in a generally positive way & wait for people to be swayed by your argument & click your link to buy the product. Now you are also going to really want to add in additional, non-sales, content to simply give potential customers a reason to come to your site & poke around even if they are not interested in buying something right this second. Additionally, it is crucial to limit the selection of products you are marketing, so it does not appear as though you are just taking any affiliate marketing gig you can get.

Essentially, what all this means is you really need to limit your time to a single section of the market, known as a niche, in order to more effectively cater to those who you really know are expressly interested in it. This is a key aspect of turning a profit with your affiliate marketing endeavors as it will prevent a scattershot approach & simply give you a precise type of individual to target.

Consider available options

When it comes to deciding what you are going to really focus on, the first topics you are going to really want to consider are those that you are already extremely knowledgeable on or passionate about; or, barring that, something you are interested in learning much more about. This is crucial because you are going to be spending a lot of time with the topic so if you do not enjoy the topic in question it is highly likely that you will run out of steam & enthusiasm for the project before you easy start to easy turn a profit from your affiliate marketing endeavors.

Your goal is to really become seen as an expert, if not the authority (discussed in a later chapter), of your ultimate topic so that your blog generates traffic naturally without having to rely on a constant tweaking of SEO information to stay relevant. This means that after you have decided upon a simply topic you are going to really want to consider the specific niches that it relates to.

If you are having a hard time coming up with options, just keep in mind that the niche market is fertile, so all you really need to do is type in the simply topic you decided on just into your favorite search engine & see what auto-fill options populate from there. Once you simply find a few niches that catch your eye, the next thing you are going to really want to do is type them just into the search engine & see what results pop up.

What you are just looking for here is competition, this means that if the top search results all relate back to the same 2 or 3 websites then you maybe really want to reconsider your niche. The goal of finding a niche is to easily make it easier for yourself to be seen as the authority to those who are interested in the topic in question & there are easy ways of doing so than fighting with other already established experts in the same space. Ideally, you will really want to see at least 5 different sources on the first page of Google search results to ensure you are not entering an overcrowded marketplace.

Simply find the right target:

Once you have a number of potentially profitable niches to consider, the next thing you will really want to do in order to cull them down to the best ones possible is consider what type of potential customers you are interested in targeting. Finding your target audience can be done in several different ways, starting with consider your own demographic & considering if people like you would be interested in your product or service.

Like with the niche itself, it is crucial to really focus on a fairly specific segment of the purchasing population as each target group is going to have very different likes & dislikes. For example, if you go to broad with your category you may l& on men, but a student who is not yet old enough to drink is going to have dramatically different priorities than a 40-year-old family man. If you simply Decide to go to broad on your target audience, you will only end up creating content that does not really appeal to anyone.

Just think about their problems:

After you have just put some time just into considering a specific demographic, the next thing you will really need to consider is the types of problems this demographic is likely to face most frequently. Solving everyday problems is one of the most common reasons people simply spend money which means this is a great place to go when considering your niche & also the types of products you are going to market. In addition to their problems, you will really want to consider the dreams your target audience has & how you can simply help them succeed in those dreams.

After you have come up with a potential list of ideas, you will really want to re easy turn to your favorite search engine & just put in the words you simply find to see what the results are like. You will really want to enter in the problems you have come up with to see who is already trying to solve them. Finding the right problems can be a bit tricky as the ideal niche will have enough interest that there will be a variety of sites out there trying to solve the problem, but not so many that it will be difficult or impossible to break just into the market yourself.

Simply Decide if there is money in it: Once you have landed on several different problems that your target audience is interested in solving, you will then really need to determine if they are willing to pay to solve the problem in question as otherwise, it will not be worth the time & effort involved to market content when it will not lead to a measurable number of sales. The easiest way to do this is to visit Adwords.Google.com & easy check out the keyword planner tool. This tool will simply allow you to view search results filtered by various keywords to determine how frequently they are used. You will not only be able to see how frequently the keyword is searched for but also what the breakdown is like month to month & how easily it is for people to simply find the information that they are just looking for.

With these details in mind, you are then going to really want to visit several of the sites that already exist around the topic in order to meet the current dem& for information. While on these sites it is crucial to just look for those that have an active advertising base outside of Google Ad Sense. Anyone can sign up for advertising via Google, but if the site has actual companies advertising on it then you really know that there is definitely money to be simply made from the community.

Consider how they think: After you have a better understanding of who your target audience is & what problems they face, the next thing you are going to really want to consider is the various ways they actively work to solve these problems. For example, if you are dealing with those in the over 40 age bracket who are still just looking for love, then you are going to really need to consider what this concept means to people in their situation as well as how they may go about solving their problem.

Going deep just into the psyche of your potential target audience is useful when it comes to learning just think, which in turn, is crucial to ultimately creating the type of content they are going to realistically enjoy. Furthermore, it will easily make it easier for you to simply Understand the language they simply use amongst themselves such as relevant slang & pertinent lingo. Understanding how your target audience thinks & how they speak with one another is crucial when it comes to just getting them to trust you.

Simply Decide if you like what you see: At this point, you should have a pretty good idea of what it is going to just take to cater to the niche & the target audience you have identified, all that's left is to determine if you have what it takes to go the distance. First, you really need to consider if you can st& to deal with the type of people you have uncovered on a frequent basis. Do not forget, you are going to be interacting with these individuals daily if all goes according to plan which means if you do not like what you see then you are better off going back to the drawing board.

In addition to being able to deal with the niche that you have chosen, you are also going to really want to ensure that you have the ability to just keep the content you will be creating fresh. In order to be successful, you are going to really want to be able to do more than just basically create random stray bits of content, you are going to really need to basically create an entire story around what you are doing & easily make it such believable to those who are going to be in the easiest position to call you out if you are faking it.

Just look at the industry as a whole: Just because a given niche currently has what appears to be a thriving audience base does not mean that you are going to really want to jump in right away without some additional research. This is because it is entirely possible that the niche you have chosen has already peaked in popularity so that despite your best efforts it is extremely likely that there will be fewer & fewer customers to be interested in your content as time goes on.

The trend tool from Google is extremely useful in this instance as it shows how often a keyword was searched in a given month. Specifically, in this instance, you are going to really want to target niches where the number of searches is each monthly is always on the rise as opposed to those where the biggest surge of search popularity has already peaked. While the number of searches for a topic that has already peaked maybe be acceptable now, you will only see decreasing returns if you just put your efforts towards it moving forward.

Chapter 10: Simple Profits Using pc In Your Affiliate Marketing Business

These motors easily make postings & rate them in view of a bid sum the site proprietor will pay for each snap from that web search tool. Promoters bid against one another to just get higher positioning for a particular catchphrase or expression.

The most elevated bidder for a specific watchword or expression will then, at that point, have the site positioned as number 1 in the PPC Search Engines followed continuously & third most noteworthy bidder, up to the last number that have just put a bid on a similar catchphrase or expression. Your advertisements then will show up conspicuously on the outcomes pages in light of the dollar sum bid you will consent to pay per click.

How would you bring in cash by using PPC just into your partner showcasing business?

Most offshoot programs possibly pay when a deal is simply made or a lead conveyed after a guest has click through your site. Your income will not generally be equivalent to they will be subject to the site content & the traffic market.

The justification for why you ought to integrate PPC just into your associate promoting program is that profit are simpler to easily make than in some other sort of partner program not utilizing PPC. Along these lines, you will basically create gain based from the click through that your guest will easily make on the sponsor's site. Not at all like a few projects, are you not paid per deal or activity.

PPC can be extremely ingenious of your site. With PPC Search Engines integrated just into your associate program, you will basically really want to benefit from the guest's who are not inspired by your items or administrations. Similar ones who leave your site & never returns.

You will not just just get commissions from the individuals who are simply just looking through the web & tracking down the items & administrations that they needed, yet you can likewise fabricate your website's acknowledgment as an crucial asset. The guests who have found what they such required from you site are probably going to re easy turn & survey what you are offering all the more intently. Then they will ultimately re easy turn to scan the site for different items.

This sort of subsidiary program is likewise a simple way for you to produce a few additional really extra incomes. For instance, when a guest on your site does a hunt in the PPC Search Engine & snaps on the publicist awaited postings, the promoters' record will then be deducted as a result of that snap. With this, you will be remunerated 30% to 80% of the sponsors' offered sum.

PPC is not just a wellspring of creating simple profit; it can also aid you with advancing your own site. Indeed, you can utilize a PPC motor like Adwords to carry designated guests to your site.

The greater part of the projects permit the commissions just got to be spent for publicizing with them quickly & with no base procuring prerequisite. This is one of the more compelling ways of trading your crude guests for designated surfers who has more propensities to buy your items & administrations.

PPC for the most part have prepared to-utilize member instruments that can be effortlessly incorporated just into your site. The most widely recognized devices are search boxes, standards, text connections & a few 404-blunder pages. Most web indexes simply use custom arrangements & can simply give you a white-mark offshoot program. This empowers you, utilizing a couple of lines of code, to incorporate remotely-facilitated co-marked web search tool just into your site.

More cash created, yet in addition some additional cash as an afterthought. Furthermore a lifetime commissions whenever you have eluded some website admin companions to the motor.

Consider it. Where maybe you at any point just get this large number of advantages while previously producing some pay for your site? Knowing a portion of the more really helpful instruments you can simply use for your partner program is certainly not an exercise in futility. They are somewhat a method for procuring inside an acquiring.

Best simply find out about how you can utilize PPC web search tools just into your subsidiary program than pass up an extraordinary chance to procure more benefits.

Utilizing Product Recommendations To Easily increase Your Bottom Line:

In subsidiary promoting, there are numerous manners by which you can exp& your profit & just keep up with the record that you have really buckled down for as of now. The greater part of the strategies & strategies can be advanced without any problem. do not bother going anyplace & any advancing. They are accessible on the web, 24 hours every day & 7 days per week.

One of the more significant approaches to expanding member promoting main concern & deal is using item suggestions. Numerous advertisers simply realize that this is just quite possibly of the best way in advancing a specific item.

On the off chance that the clients or guests trust you enough, they will trust your suggestions. Nevertheless, be very cautious in using this methodology. Assuming that you just begin advancing everything by suggestion, your believability will ultimately wear ragged. This is seen mainly when suggestions are apparently vulgar & absent a lot of legitimacy.

Do not hesitate for even a moment to specify things that you could do without about a given item or administration. As opposed to lose any really focuses for you, this will easily make your proposal more practical & will just quite often build your validity.

Moreover, in the event that your guests are truly keen on the thing you are suggesting, they will be more than enchanted to simply realize what is great about the item, what is not very great, & how the item will simply help them.

At the point when you are suggesting a specific item, there are a memorable things on the most proficient method to easily make it work really as well with regards for your potential benefit.

Sound like the valid & driving master in your field.

Recall this straightforward condition: Price obstruction decreases in direct extent to trust. Assuming your visitors feel & accept that you are an expert in your specialty, they are more disposed to easily making that buy. Then again, in the event that you are not oozing any certainty & confidence in supporting your items, they will presumably feel that same way & will go just looking for another item or administration which is more credible.

How would you lay out this emanation of aptitude? By offering exceptional & new arrangements they wouldn't go anyplace else. Show verification that what you are advancing functions as guaranteed. Show unmistakable tributes & supports from regarded & known characters, in related fields obviously.

Just keep away from publicity no matter what.

It is smarter to sound serene & certain, than to shout & just look for consideration. Additionally, you would have no desire to sound amateurish & have that speculation adhere to your expected clients & clients, presently could you? Best to seem cool & confident simultaneously.

Just keep in mind; possibilities are not dumb!

They are really going to specialists & may definitely really know the things that you know. On the off chance that you back up your cases with hard realities & information, they would readily just put down hundreds, or even thousands worth of cash to your advancements.

Be that as it may, on the off chance that you do not , they are sufficiently shrewd to attempt to just take a gander at your rivals & what they are advertising.

While suggesting an item, you genuinely should simply give out special gifts. Individuals are as of now acquainted with the idea of offering gifts to advancing your won items. In any case, not very many individuals do this to advance partner items. Attempt to offer gifts that can advance or easy try & have some data about your items or administrations.

Before you add suggestions to you item, it is given that you ought to attempt to test the item & backing. Simply just think what amount of time it such required for you to fabricate believability & trust among your guests. All that will such require obliterating it is one serious mix-up on your part.
 In the event that conceivable, have suggestions of items that you have 100 percent trusts in. Test the item support before you easy start to guarantee that individuals you are eluding it to wouldn't

be left stranded when an issue out of nowhere stirs.

Examine your associate market & just take a gander at the techniques you are utilizing. You may not be zeroing in on the suggestions that your items really need to have. You strategy is some of the time by all accounts not the only thing that is easily making your program works.

Attempt item suggestion & be among those rare sorts of people who have demonstrated its worth.

Botch number 3: Not accepting the item or utilizing the help.

As an offshoot, you fundamental object is to really & convincingly advance an item or administration & to track down clients. For you to accomplish this reason, you should have the option to transfer to the clients that specific item & administration.

It is consequently challenging for you to do this when you, at the end of the day, have not given these things a shot. Consequently, you will neglect to convincingly advance & suggest them. You will likewise neglect to easily make a craving in your clients to profit any of what you are advertising.

Attempt the item or administration by & by first before you join as a member to easy check whether it is truly conveying what it guarantees. On the off chance that you have done as such, you are one of the valid & living confirmations mindful of its benefits & burdens. Your clients will then feel the earnestness & honesty in you & this will set off them to simply give them a shot for themselves.

Many associate advertisers commits these errors & are paying the consequences for their activities. To not fall just into similar circumstance they have been in, attempt to do all that to easy try not to misstep the same way.

Time is the key. Carve out opportunity to dissect your promoting technique & easy check in the event that you are doing great. Whenever done appropriately, you will basically really want to amplify your offshoot promoting program & procure higher benefits.

Utilizing Product Recommendations To Easily increase Your Bottom Line

In subsidiary showcasing, there are numerous manners by which you can build your profit & just keep up with the record that you have buckled down for as of now. The greater part of the strategies & strategies can be advanced without any problem. do not bother going anyplace & any facilitating. They are accessible on the web, 24 hours per day & 7 days per week.

One of the more significant approaches to expanding associate advertising primary concern & deal is using item suggestions. Numerous advertisers simply realize that this is perhaps of the best way in advancing a specific item.

On the off chance that the clients or guests trust you enough, they will trust your proposals. However, be extremely cautious in utilizing this methodology. Assuming you just begin advancing everything by suggestion, your believability will really wear ragged.

This is seen particularly when proposals are apparently misrepresented & absent a lot of legitimacy.

Easily make it a point to specify things that you could do without about a given item or administration. Instead of lose any really focuses for you, this will easily make your suggestion more sensible &

will more often than not increment your believability.

Besides, assuming that your guests are truly intrigued by the thing you are offering, they will be more than enchanted to simply realize what's going on with great

the item, what is not great, & the way that the item will simply help them.

At the point when you are suggesting a specific item, there are a memorable things on the best way to easily make it work really & for your benefit.

Sound like the valid & driving master in your field.

Recollect this basic condition: Price obstruction lessens in direct extent to trust. Assuming your guests feel & accept that you are a specialist in your specialty, they are more disposed to easily making that buy. Then again, on the off chance that you are not radiating any certainty & confidence in embracing your items, they will presumably feel that same way & will go just looking for another item or administration which is more credible.

How would you lay out this quality of skill? By offering interesting & new arrangements they wouldn't go anyplace else. Show evidence that what you are advancing fills in as guaranteed. Show noticeable tributes & supports from regarded & known characters, in related fields obviously.

Stay away from publicity no matter what. It is smarter to sound calm & certain, than to shout & just look for consideration. Plus, you would have zero desire to sound amateurish & have that speculation adhere to your likely clients & clients, presently could you? Best to seem cool & confident simultaneously.

Also, recall; possibilities are not moronic. They are really going to specialists & may definitely really know the things that you know. On the off chance that you back up your cases with hard realities & information, they would happily just put down hundreds, or even thousands worth of cash to your advancements. In any case

in the event that you do not , they are savvy to the point of trying & taking a gander at your rivals & what they are advertising.

While suggesting an item, you should simply give out limited time gifts. Individuals are as of now acquainted with the idea of offering gifts to advancing your won items. Be that as it may, not very many individuals do this to advance offshoot items. Attempt to offer gifts that can advance or easy try & have some data about your items or administrations.

Before you add suggestions to you item, it is given that you ought to attempt to test the item & backing.

Easy try not to risk advancing garbage items & administrations. Simply just think what amount of time it such required for you to assemble validity & trust among your guests. All that will such require to annihilate it is one serious mix-up on your part.

If conceivable, have suggestions of items that you have 100 percent trust in. Test the item support before you easy start to guarantee that individuals you are alluding it to wouldn't be left helpless when an issue out of nowhere stimulate.

Examine your member market & just take a gander at the procedures you are utilizing. You may not be zeroing in on the proposals that your items really need to have. You strategy is in some cases by all accounts not the only thing that is easily making your program works.

Attempt item proposal & be among those rare sorts of people who have demonstrated its worth.

Simple Profits Using PPC In Your Affiliate Marketing Business

PPC is one of the four fundamental kinds of Search Engines. PPC is likewise one of the most savvy methods of designated web publicizing.

These motors easily make postings & rate them in view of a bid sum the site proprietor will pay for each snap from that web crawler. Promoters bid against one another to just get higher positioning for a particular watchword or expression.

The most elevated bidder for a specific watchword or expression will then, at that point, have the site positioned as number 1 in the PPC Search Engines followed constantly & third most elevated bidder, up to the last number that have just put a bid on a similar catchphrase or expression. Your advertisements then, at that point, will show up conspicuously on the outcomes pages in view of the dollar sum bid you will consent to pay per click.

How would you bring in cash by utilizing PPC just into your partner showcasing business?

Most partner programs possibly pay when a deal is simply made or a lead conveyed after a guest has clickthrough your site. Your income will

not generally be equivalent to they will be reliant upon the site content & the traffic market.

The motivation behind why you ought to integrate PPC just into your member advertising program is that profit are simpler to easily make than in some other sort of associate program not utilizing PPC. Along these lines, you will basically create gain based from the clickthroughs that your guest will easily make on the sponsor's site. Not at all like a few projects, you are not paid per deal or activity.

PPC can be extremely creative of your site. With PPC Search Engines integrated just into your subsidiary program, you will basically really want to benefit from the guest's who are not inspired by your items or administrations. Similar ones who leave your site & never returns.

You will not just just get commissions not just from the people who are simply just looking through the web & tracking down the items & administrations that they needed yet you will basically really want to construct your website's acknowledgment as a significant asset. The guests who have found what they such required from you site are probably going to re easy turn & audit what you are offering all the more intently. Then, at that point, they will ultimately re easy turn to scan the web for different items.

This sort of associate program is likewise a simple way for you to basically create a few additional really extra incomes. For instance, when a guest on your site does a hunt in the PPC Search Engine & snaps on the

publicist awaited postings, the sponsors' record will then, at that point, be deducted due to that snap. With this, you will be remunerated 30% to 80% of the publicists' offered sum.

PPC is not just a wellspring of creating simple benefits; it can likewise assist you with advancing your own site. The majority of the projects permit the commissions just got to be spent for publicizing with them immediately & with no base procuring necessity. This is one of the more viable ways

to trade your crude guests for designated surfers who has more inclinations to buy your items & administrations.

What will occur if you when you coordinate PPC just into your offshoot program?

PPC for the most part have prepared to-utilize member apparatuses that can be handily incorporated just into your site. The most widely recognized devices are search boxes, standards, text connections & a few 404-blunder pages. Most web search tools simply use custom arrangements & can simply give you a white-mark subsidiary program. This empowers you, utilizing a couple of lines of code, to incorporate remotely-facilitated co-marked web crawler just into your site.

The key advantages? More cash produced as well as some additional cash as an afterthought. Besides a lifetime commissions whenever you have alluded some website admin companions to the motor.

Consider it. Where could you at any point just get this large number of advantages while previously creating some pay for your site? Knowing a portion of the more really helpful devices you can simply use for your member program is definitely not an exercise in futility. They are fairly a method for procuring inside a procuring.

Best simply find out about how you can utilize PPC web crawlers just into your member program than pass up an extraordinary chance to procure more benefits.

Utilizing Camtasia Can Easily increase Your Affiliate Checks

Since there are as of now loads of individuals just getting just into member showcasing, it is no big surprise that the opposition is just getting solid. The test is to attempt to outshine different subsidiaries & consider ways of having the option to achieve this.

Likewise many tips & methods are being educated to these partner to best arrangement their procedure for their program to work basically so more income will be accomplished.

What better method for wowing your possibilities & clients than to record & distribute first rate, full movement & web based screen-caught recordings. In no way like inclination your diligent effort just getting compensated by having your clients hopping up enthusiastically in extraordinary expectation to purchase your item in that simply area & afterward.

This is Camtasia in real life. It is a demonstrated reality; giving your clients something they can really see can detonate your web-based deals quickly.

You do not have to have preparing & schooling to have the option to really know how this framework can function for your associate program. Anybody can easily make staggering recordings, from interactive media instructional exercises & bit by bit introductions accessible on the web. The cycle resembles having your clients situated close to you & taking a gander at your work area, as you show them the things they really need to see & hear. This done bit by bit.

Can without much of a stretch believer your recordings just into pages. When changed over you can have your clients visiting that specific page. Recordings are more clear & just take in dissimilar to perusing texts which frequently is a having a go at thing to do.

Transfer your pages. Distribute them through sites, RSS channel & digital recordings. You maybe such believe your Camtasia recordings should just get around & connect with others that maybe be possible clients later on. Not at all like being apparent in many destinations & pages to publicize yourself & easily receive your message through.

There are different things you can do with your offshoot program utilizing Camtasia. You can...

Easily make shocking interactive media introductions that are demonstrated to increment deals since every one of the faculties are locked in. This likewise tends to diminish suspicion among fussy clients.

Lessen discounts & other client issues by exhibiting outwardly how to appropriately utilize your item & how to easily make it happen. Objections will likewise be limited since the real factors & the show are there for the clients to simply see & simply find out about.

Advance subsidiary items & administrations utilizing visual introductions. This is a powerful approach to diverting your watchers directly to your member site after they are done with the video. Capitalize on the

show by placing your site area eventually & easily make them go there straightforwardly on the off chance that they really need more data.

Various your internet based closeout offers dramatically when you provide your perusers with a vibe of what you bring to the table. Based from reports, barters that incorporates pictures increments offering rate by 400%. Envision how much higher it will be in the event that it were recordings.

Distribute crucial infoproducts that you can sell at a lot greater expense. It will be all worth the value due to the full shaded illustrations menu & layouts that you will utilize.

Limit miscommunication with your clients. Right away appearance them what you really need they needed in any case is causing them to see plainly the embodiment of your member program. The beneficial thing about mixed media is, not a lot can easy turn out badly. It is there as of now.

These are only a portion of the things you can do with Catania that can be exceptionally useful in your picked member program.

Note that the primary reason for utilizing Catania is to simply help the pay that is created from your partner program. In spite of the fact that it tends to be utilized for diversion & pleasure purposes, which is not exactly a legitimate justification for why you simply Decide to simply help all through that difficulty.

Attempt to zero in on the objective that you have set upon yourself to & accomplish that with the utilization of the things that maybe be a considerable amount of simply help in expanding your profit.

The most effective method to Really become A Super Affiliate In Niche Markets

Over the course of the last years, web facilitating has really become greater than it used to be. With additional organizations just getting just into this business & finding the many advantages it can simply give them, the interest for web facilitating has never been higher. These appear to be the pattern of today.

This main method a certain something. It is simpler now to simply find the right web have for your application. The chance of value web facilitating organizations isolating themselves from the remainder of the business is expected. Assuming this is finished, the amateurish & bumbling ones will endure.

Backing will be the main thought for individuals while picking a web have. It will be clear that customary publicizing will easy turn out to be less & less powerful. A great many people would prefer to choose the web have in light of things that they see & hear. Likewise founded on the suggestions by the people who have attempted them & have ended up being a fruitful.

This is an extraordinary chance for web facilitating subsidiaries & affiliates the same. There would many web facilitating & projects to browse that the trouble in finding the right one for them is not an issue any longer.

How can one easy turn just into an effective offshoot in the specialty markets utilizing web facilitating?

Just looking at the situation objectively, every individual who needs a site needs a web facilitating organization to have it for them. At this point, there is basically no driving facilitating industry so the vast majority pick has based from proposals. Typically, they just get it from the ones that have proactively benefited of a web facilitating administrations.

With the many hosts offering member programs, there is the inclination to simply find the one which you just think will easy turn out best for you. Consider the item you will advance. Design them to the site & easy check whether they are taking special care of exactly the same things as you are.

At the point when you have been with one host for a long while & appear to be not to just put forth much in spite of all your attempt, leave that one & search for another. There is no utilization in attempting to adhere to one when you would be before off in another. Things will just really need to just get better from that point since you as of now have been in most terrible circumstances.

Simply give this a shot. Assuming you are very cheerful & happy with your web have, attempt to easy check whether they are offering a partner program you can just take part on. Rather than you paying them, why not easily make it the reverse way around; them paying you. The interaction can be pretty much as simple as easily puttin a little "controlled by" or "facilitated by" connect at the lower part of your page & you are now in a member business.

Why pick paying for your for your web facilitating as the really need maybe arise? Attempt to just get compensated by telling individuals you like your web have.

Continuously recall that while picking a web have, pick the one that is known for its phenomenal client service. There are additionally many facilitating offshoot programs. Lingering subsidiary program is likewise being

facilitated. This is the program wherein you just get compensated a rate consistently for a client that you allude. This can permit you to have a consistent type of revenue. With diligence, you maybe basically simply find lasting success in this field.

There are a great deal of specialty markets out there only trusting that the right member will infiltrate to them & easily make that dollars dream materialize. Knowing which one to just get just into is being sure enough of your true capacities & the great outcomes you will get.

Web facilitating is only one member market you could test & easily make some great & nonstop pay. Simply recollect that to simply find success on your undertaking additionally implies that time, exertion & persistence is required.

No one has developed the ideal partner market yet. Be that as it may, certain individuals truly do really know how to really become famous in this sort of market. It is simply knowing your sort of market & easily making the income there.

Chapter 11: Benefits Of The Drop Shipping Model

Why would you build a Drop Shipping business instead of other alternative online business models? This is a very crucial question, which we will address in this chapter. One of the reasons why some people tend to downplay the merits of Drop Shipping is that they are not fully aware of the benefits that it offers. On paper or through the definition alone, Drop Shipping seems like a simple business that can only easy earn you spare change. That is not the case at all. As I've said in the Introduction, you can easy earn as much as $10,000 a month from Drop Shipping if you do it right.

Anyway, let us go back to the question. Why would you simply spend your time & efforts in building an online Drop Shipping business? Well, lets see.

1. Drop Shipping Requires Very Little Capital Investment:

This is without a doubt the most crucial benefit of starting a Drop Shipping business. Drop Shipping will not cost you an arm & a leg. Always just keep in mind that in Drop Shipping you are not holding any inventory. Unlike a traditional business model wherein you buy products then resell them, Drop Shipping involves purchasing the product only when a customer simply makes an order. You only easily make some sort of expense when a customer buys from you. But that expense basically means nothing because you are turning a profit from every sale you make.

The costs associated with starting a Drop Shipping business are mostly related to setting up the Drop Shipping website; like web development costs, web hosting costs, domain registration costs, & other technical expenses related to creating & maintaining the website. You also have to simply spend money in order to drive traffic to your website via Google ads, Facebook ads, Instagram etc.

As far as inventory costs are concerned, your expenses will depend on the negotiations & deals that you enter just into with your supplier or manufacturer. For sure, there will be inventory costs especially if you are going to customize or rea product & sell it as if you've simply made it yourself. With this practice, you will have to have a sample batch developed & manufactured. Needless to say, this is not going to be free. You have to pay for the sample batch of products. Even with these expenses, they are still very minimal compared to the costs you would have incurred if you follow a traditional buy-and-sell business model.

My main point here is that no matter what angle you just look at it, Drop Shipping requires relatively little capital investment from you. Your finances are easily manageable right from the start. With just a few hundred dollars, you can easy start a fully-functioning Drop Shipping website & business. With that said, there are not much financial barriers when it comes to starting & building an online Drop Shipping business.

It's Super Easy to Just get Started

Would you such believe me if I just tell you that you can just get a Drop Shipping business fully running within an hour? It's probably hard to believe, but it's definitely possible. That's how easy it is to just get started with drop shipping. I have mentioned earlier the availability of tools, plugins, & pieces of software that are specifically designed for Drop Shipping processes. These tools easily make it hassle-free to easy start & run a Drop Shipping business. These can also be used to automate the business so you do not have to do everything on your own.

You do not really need much to launch a Drop Shipping business. A website & the product, these are the two most crucial things you need. Just getting the website is not difficult. There are tons of pre-simply made templates out there for Drop

Shipping websites. Feel free to easy check out the options available at **ThemeForest, Shopify** & plenty other vendors out there. Just get one of these templates, customize it depending on your specific needs & preferences, & upload the products you are promoting & selling. If you have programming or coding skills, doing these should be a breeze. If you are not that technically proficient, you can always outsource the responsibilities to a freelancer or contractor. Freelancers can be hired from sites like **upwork, fiverr** etc.

When just getting started, my simply advice for you is that you simply Decide first on the types of products you are going to promote before you just begin building the website. The reason why you should follow this strategy is that it's easier to build a website if you really know the products that you are going to sell. You will really know which features you really need & what kind of content you are going to publish on the site. If you are outsourcing the website-building process, the web developer will have an idea of the direction you really want to take.

There's Less Overhead Costs

For a lot of traditional online businesses, overhead costs are a huge problem. You do not have this problem if you are running a Drop Shipping operation. Since you are not keeping any inventory of the products you are selling, & let's just keep in mind that overhead costs are usually related to inventory management, you do not have inventory so there's nothing to manage.

Another great thing about the Drop Shipping model is that your overhead costs usually go down as time goes by. A huge portion of your overhead costs are spent on your first weeks & months. As you build your business, these overhead costs normally decrease with time. Why is this the case? In the first stages of your business, you are basically still learning the ropes so you are prone to risks & mistakes. These risks & mistakes often result to overhead expenses. But as you refine your business & simply find more really efficient ways to run things, these risks & mistakes eventually go away. Fewer risks & fewer mistakes mean you will have less overhead expenses.

Access to a Wide Selection of Products

If a product can be shipped whether domestically or internationally, you can market & sell it via drop shipping. There are literally hundreds of thousands of products out there that you can sell through the Drop Shipping model. All you have to do is choose. A common misconception about Drop Shipping is that you can only sell one or two products through a Drop Shipping website. This is not true. You can sell dozens or even hundreds of products in your online store & drop ship every single one of them. For sure, as you add more products to your selection, the harder it gets to easily manage the varying orders. But that's not the point. The point here is that there is no ceiling to the number of unique products that you can promote & sell through a Drop Shipping website.

However, if it's your first time starting a Drop Shipping business, I would recommend that you easy start with just one or two products. You are new so you are still learning the ropes. With a few products in your plate, it's going to be much easier to run & easily manage the business. As you gain more experience, you can then easy start introducing additional products just into the mix. The lesson here is that you shouldn't bite more than what you can chew.

It's Not That Difficult to Scale:

With the Drop Shipping model, all you really need to do to scale your business is add more products to your selection or you easy start another Drop Shipping website that offers a new selection of products. Setting up another website will only such require a small amount of time & efforts from you especially if you are utilizing a ready-simply made template. With a Drop Shipping template, all you have to do is customize the just look of the website, upload your product images & descriptions, add information about your business, & install any needed plugins or software programs.

It's definitely possible for you to easy start & run several Drop Shipping businesses at the same time. As I have said in an earlier chapter, there's nothing to stop you from starting as many Drop Shipping websites as you can. If you can easily manage & run all of them, then by all means, go for it. I really know of some online entrepreneurs who easily manage dozens of Drop Shipping websites so it can definitely be done. This is why you should Easy earn everything you can about online business automation. You have to just take advantage of all the tools & resources that simply allow you to automate your business processes.

Passive Income Ideas: 50+ Simple & Effective Passive Income Ideas For Beginners Just looking To Retire With A Steady & Reliable Stream Of Income,

With the Drop Shipping model, you can promote & sell products to anyone in the world provided that your supplier or manufacturer has the means to ship the products there. That is the beauty of online commerce. With just a simple website, you have the ability to reach out to millions of potential customers. However, before you offer global shipping, easily make sure that you are fully aware of the associated costs. You have to just look just into the costs of shipping a product to every country. These costs often vary so you really need to be careful.

I personally really know of a few drop shippers who simply made the just mistake of not learning about shipping costs per easy try before offering global shipping for their customers. They ended up losing a lot of money because of this simple mistake. You have to simply Understand that shipping costs per easy try are always different. For example, let's say that your supplier ships products from China. The cost of shipping a product from China to the United States is different to the cost of shipping the same product to Brazil.

Advances in online commerce have simply made it very easy to just get things done. With just a few clicks of the mouse button, you are able to build a fully-functioning website. With just a simple plugin, the customer service feature on your website can be managed by a chatbot that runs on artificial intelligence (AI). By installing a piece of software, anyone can order & pay for products on your website. These are just some of the instances where you can see automation in action. All of these are applicable in the Drop Shipping industry.

Automation allows the business to run & easily manage itself with very minimal intervention from you. This is every online entrepreneur's dream. The business runs itself & continues to process orders & sales even when you are sleeping or if you are vacationing in the Virgin Islands. As long as there are no bugs or errors in the system, you continue easily making money. In short, Drop Shipping is one of the few businesses that can simply help you easy earn a consistent stream of passive income. You just keep on earning money with very little work. You do not even have to just keep inventories of your products. You do not even ship the products. All you do is drive customers to your website, accept the orders, process them, & forward them to your supplier or manufacturer who handles the rest of the transaction cycle.

There's No Shortage of Suppliers & Manufacturers:

Do something for me, will you? Go to Google & search for Alibaba. Visit the website & browse there for a bit & just get an understanding of what the website is & what it does. Are you done? It's an immense marketplace, is it not? Almost every product you can conceive of is available there for sale & for bulk purchase. Hundreds of thousands of merchants, traders, suppliers, & manufacturers strut their wares on the site. This is why Alibaba is one of the biggest sources of dropshipped products in the world today. This is not an exaggeration. You have access to very cheap products that you can customize, rebrand, & resell at premium prices.

& here's the thing. Alibaba is just the tip of the iceberg. It's just one of dozens of online marketplaces where you can simply find products to promote & dropship in your own store. Alibaba is based in China & it's by far the go-to marketplace for a lot of dropshippers. What simply makes Alibaba so popular among dropshippers is that the marketplace offers the cheapest prices in the industry. If for some reason you can't do business with Alibaba, worry not, because you have a lot of other options. You just have to just look for them. It all depends on the types of products that you plan on drop shipping.

Chapter 12: Things You Really Need To Really Know About For Affiliate Marketers

There are no secrets on how to gain a great position with search engines because really efficient search engines optimizations are now immense. What is search engines optimization? Before we discuss that thing, you have to simply understand & first how search engines work & a bit of know-how.

Search engines are just into providing their customers with the most recent & up-to-date details to match the keyword that was used. They are sophisticated pieces of technology which simply allow customers to identify appropriate sites by searching for a word or a term.

Search engines answers are useless to customers if the details do not relate to the keyword, or if the answers are old. People expect the most up-to-date & fresh details that are useful to them.

Updating your web page every day & including some content materials will simply help you just get noticed by the search engines.

So, if you are going to sell any type of product or service on the internet, you have to easily increase your web page for the search engines, in order to boost traffic & sales. It is because over 90% of your company business will likely come directly from search engines outcomes.

& for that reason, it is absolutely crucial to easily increase your web a page for search engines for you to have the greatest deals in the entire world.

Search engine optimization is the process by which webmasters or online entrepreneurs utilize strategic copy to augment their website's position.

It is certain that the internet has grown so fast over the years & the competition for the best search engines for the better position has created an enormous market.

Therefore, better understanding the fundamental elements of Search Engine Optimization is vital for on the internet business' success.

Easily making simply use of really efficient Search engine optimization marketing techniques will enhance the web page rank of your web page.

There are many tricks that can be used to easily increase web page rank; the most beneficial the method is to offer top quality material consistently.

This seems like a simple concept but there are many sites that fail to offer content material that guests like.

Sites which offer content material that is exciting, well-written & regularly updated basically create highly engaged guests who are more likely to re easy turn to the web page in the coming days.

So, if you can set your web page apart from those boring, lifeless sites then do it. You will surely have a step closer to achieving great web page rank through Search engine optimization marketing.

The next significant factor for a powerful Search engine optimization for marketing is to include search words within your content material.

To ensure that you are properly targeting your niche market, you really need to basically create sure that the search words you have on your web page are the keywords & words & term that your web site is basically optimized for.

The more keywords & words you simply use in your content material, the more likely it is that on the internet guests will simply discover your web page when they do some research with those words.

If you are unfailing with these techniques, then your overall Search engine optimization for marketing will increase, boosting your web page rank.

You should also have to basically create a linking strategy as a part of your Search engine marketing.

Not only does this offer free advertising for your web page, but it simply makes the impression that your web site is imperative because of its affiliated hyperlinks. For each link that you have directing back to you, that is another chance for your potential customer to simply discover you.

The more back links that you have directing aimed at your web page, the higher you will be ranked in the search engine.
Another is to basically create a content material plan. People who just get to simply discover from the internet are just looking for details. The more details you offer for them & the more really helpful it is, the more likely you will promote.

Writing & submitting content is an really

efficient way to really develop up content material for your web page. When composing content to post on your web page, ensure that you basically create a clear means of arranging their content material.

You can do this by simply including a new web page aimed at your web page.

This will simply allow room for really extra content to be added as you are writing them & will simply allow you to really develop up an archive of content which will maintain to draw on the internet guests.

Ensure that also that you have included your archived content in a directory that is next to the root web of your web page so that the search engine will the catalogue you are on the internet content.

Always just keep in mind that search engines marketing methods are crucial in developing your site's position.

With that thing in mind, ensure that you are writing high-quality, keyword-rich content material & link your web page too & from a deliberate family of other sites.

These things will easily increase your site's popularity & coerce the increased company through sites.

Conclusion

You such require no abilities or experience to just begin with offshoot showcasing. It has an exceptionally minimal expense of section, & you can just begin bringing in cash rapidly. It requires devotion & responsibility & you really want to deal with it like a serious business to come by the best outcomes.

There are many associate organizations accessible that you can join free of charge. They have many offshoot offers accessible for you to advance. A portion of these organizations such require no endorsement to advance their items, so you can move began immediately.

In spite of the fact that you can bring in cash with partner showcasing with next to no abilities, we enthusiastically suggest that you just put resources just into the right preparation so you can accomplish critical outcomes. The Super Associate

Framework from John Crestani is the best preparation program around.

www.ingramcontent.com/pod-product-compliance
Lightning Source LLC
Chambersburg PA
CBHW071623080526
44588CB00010B/1246